BUBBLES

by Meg Gaertner

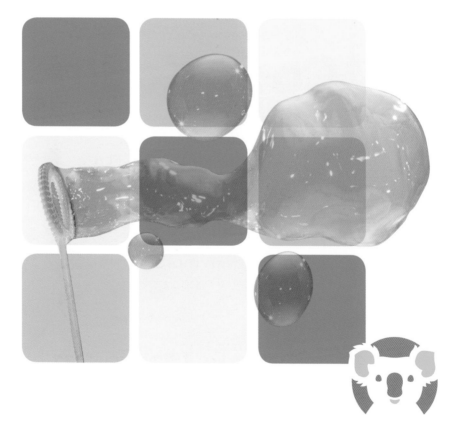

Cody Koala

An Imprint of Pop!

popbooksonline.com

abdobooks.com

Published by Pop!, a division of ABDO, PO Box 398166, Minneapolis, Minnesota 55439. Copyright © 2020 by POP, LLC. International copyrights reserved in all countries. No part of this book may be reproduced in any form without written permission from the publisher. Pop!™ is a trademark and logo of POP, LLC.

Printed in the United States of America, North Mankato, Minnesota

052019
092019

THIS BOOK CONTAINS RECYCLED MATERIALS

Cover Photo: iStockphoto
Interior Photos: iStockphoto, 1; Shutterstock Images, 5, 7 (top), 7 (bottom middle), 7 (bottom right), 7 (bottom left), 9 (top), 9 (bottom left), 9 (bottom right), 13, 14, 17, 19, 20; Red Line Editorial, 10–11

Editor: Brienna Rossiter
Series Designer: Sarah Taplin

Library of Congress Control Number: 2018964772

Publisher's Cataloging-in-Publication Data

Names: Gaertner, Meg, author.
Title: Bubbles / by Meg Gaertner.
Description: Minneapolis, Minnesota : Pop!, 2020 | Series: Science all around | Includes online resources and index.
Identifiers: ISBN 9781532163555 (lib. bdg.) | ISBN 9781532164996 (ebook)
Subjects: LCSH: Bubbles--Juvenile literature. | Soap bubbles--Juvenile literature. | Science--Juvenile literature.
Classification: DDC 530.427--dc23

Hello! My name is

Cody Koala

Pop open this book and you'll find QR codes like this one, loaded with information, so you can learn even more!

Scan this code* and others like it while you read, or visit the website below to make this book pop.

popbooksonline.com/bubbles

*Scanning QR codes requires a web-enabled smart device with a QR code reader app and a camera.

Table of Contents

Chapter 1

Blowing Bubbles

A girl blows into her bubble wand. The air she blows gets trapped in a layer of soapy water. It forms bubbles. The bubbles are shaped like **spheres**. They float in the air.

Watch a video here!

Bubbles are made of water and soap. One thin layer of water rests between two thin layers of soap.

Sometimes when light hits a bubble's layers, a rainbow appears.

Chapter 2

Molecules

Bubbles happen when soap mixes with water. Water is made of many tiny **molecules**. Water molecules all have the same shape.

Complete an activity here!

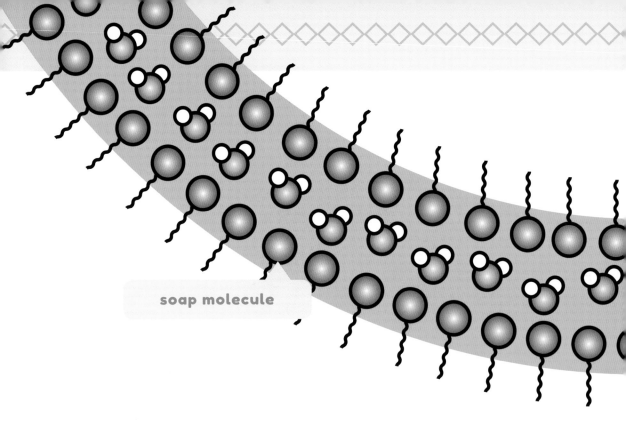

soap molecule

Soap is also made of molecules. One end of a soap molecule is attracted to water.

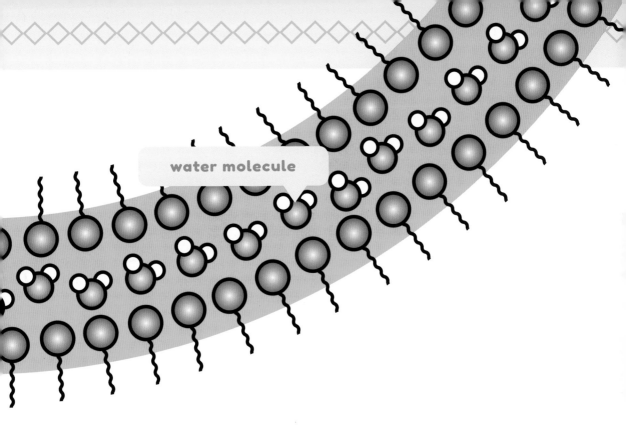

water molecule

It points toward water.
The other end of a soap
molecule points away
from water.

Chapter 3

Surface Tension

Water **molecules** are joined by strong **bonds**. The bonds help them stick together. They also create **surface tension**.

Learn more here!

Think of a glass of water. The glass holds many molecules. Most are surrounded by other water molecules. They pull on one another from all sides.

Molecules at the surface of the glass have no water above them. Most water is below them. And some water molecules are to the sides. Molecules at the surface are pulled toward these other water molecules. They will not easily move up or away.

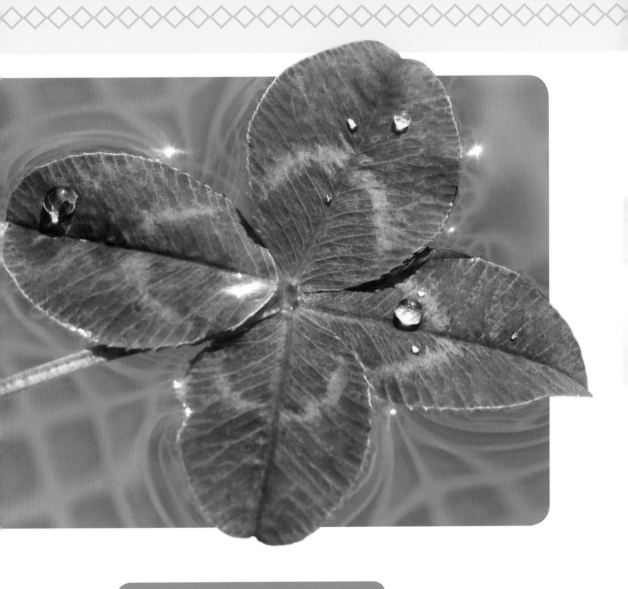

Surface tension lets some objects float on the water.

Chapter 4

Pop!

When soap and water mix,
the soap **molecules** pull
on the water molecules.
Surface tension decreases.
The water molecules stretch
away from one another.
A bubble forms.

Learn more here!

Bubbles do not last long.

They have thin layers.

The layers break easily.

When they break,
the bubble pops.

Some bubbles pop when the water inside them **evaporates**.

Making Connections

Text-to-Self

Have you ever blown bubbles? How long did the bubbles last? Did they float or fall?

Text-to-Text

Have you read other books about molecules? What did you learn?

Text-to-World

Bubbles have the shape of a sphere. What other sphere-shaped objects can you think of?

Glossary

bond – a connection that makes two things stick together.

evaporate – to change from a liquid to a gas.

molecule – one of the smallest bits that matter can be broken into.

sphere – a round, ball-like shape.

surface tension – a force that causes the molecules at a liquid's surface to pull together and form a stretchy layer.

Index

Online Resources

popbooksonline.com

Thanks for reading this Cody Koala book!

Scan this code* and others like it in this book, or visit the website below to make this book pop!

popbooksonline.com/bubbles

*Scanning QR codes requires a web-enabled smart device with a QR code reader app and a camera.